CW01424735

Yours sincerely

Church Times Study Guides

Deliver Us: Exploring the Problem of Evil
Mike Higton

Doing What Comes Naturally? The Christian Tradition and Sexual Ethics
Neil Messer

Embracing the Day: Exploring Daily Prayer
Stephen Burns

Faith Under Fire: Exploring 1 Peter and Revelation
John Holdsworth

The Fellowship of the Three: Exploring the Trinity
Jane Williams

Here is the News!
John Holdsworth

Immersed in Grace: Exploring the Baptism
Stephen Burns

Living the Thanksgiving: Exploring the Eucharist
Stephen Burns

The Mighty Tortoise: Exploring the Church
Jane Williams

Prophets and Loss: Exploring the Old Testament
John Holdsworth

The Same But Different: The Synoptic Gospels
John Holdsworth

Who Do You Say that I Am? Exploring Our Images of Jesus
Jane Williams

Yours Sincerely: Exploring the Letters of the New Testament
John Holdsworth

Church Times Study Guide

Yours Sincerely

Exploring the Letters of the New Testament

John Holdsworth

CANTERBURY
PRESS
Norwich

© John Holdsworth 2007

First published in 2007 by the Canterbury Press Norwich
(a publishing imprint of Hymns Ancient & Modern Limited,
a registered charity)
9–17 St Alban's Place, London N1 0NX

www.scm-canterburypress.co.uk

All rights reserved. No part of this publication may be
reproduced, stored in a retrieval system, or transmitted,
in any form or by any means, electronic, mechanical,
photocopying or otherwise, without the prior permission of
the publisher, Canterbury Press

Scripture quotations are from the Revised Standard Version of the
Bible, copyright 1946, 1952 and 1971 by the Division of Christian
Education of the National Council of the Churches of Christ in the
USA. Used by permission. All rights reserved.

British Library Cataloguing in Publication data

A catalogue record for this book is available
from the British Library

ISBN 978-1-85311-774-9
5-pack ISBN 978-1-85311-775-6

Typeset by Regent Typesetting, London
Printed and bound by Gallpen Colour Print, Norwich

Contents

Leaders' Notes

Planning sessions

Remember

Keep in mind the ethos: 'The course is an attempt to share, not to talk down.'

There is enough material and exercises to offer a choice if you are having a single session: familiarize yourself with all material and select.

Prioritize

Choose the most important aims for your group. Deciding which aims to focus on will help you select the most appropriate material and exercises.

Decide the balance, in your local context, between learning aims relating to the course content and other needs (e.g. enabling people to meet socially, encouraging people to speak about faith). This also helps selecting appropriate material and process.

Planning

Have a variety of different ways of working – e.g. discussion in twos or threes, discussion all together in plenary, one person talking, personal reflection, opportunities to write down etc. Changing the pace aids concentration. Also people have different learning styles, and sessions are likely to work best if they include elements that cater to the variety of ways in which people learn.

Plan how the group will work through your chosen exercises. There are many ways of using the material.

When introducing new concepts or material, think whether there is any additional background information that might help people without much prior knowledge.

Decide what prayer/worship opportunities to include. Some may find it practical to have optional worship beforehand: others might want something that contrasts with the 'wordiness' of discussion.

Let participants know if they need to bring anything with them, or if you want them to do anything before the session.

Getting started

Sitting comfortably

A circle rather than rows encourages discussion/participation. Arrange seating so all can see each other's faces.

Forming the group

Make sure everybody knows who everyone is, and introduce the purpose of the session. Explain how it will be shaped and the time when it will end (make sure you finish then!). Using a quick introductory exercise can give each person an opportunity to give his or her name and say something. Give limit for contributions (e.g. 'one sentence'); otherwise they tend to get longer going round the circle.

Ground-rules/Boundaries/Group covenants

It helps if all are clear and agreed on how the group will run at the beginning. You may want to suggest a few 'ground rules' (e.g. not interrupting/confidentiality) and give the group a chance to suggest others.

ix

Group facilitation

The leader/facilitator needs to attend to the dynamics and smooth working of the group, as well as the course material. Maintaining the group needs skills of encouragement and 'gate-keeping' to help people get involved and keep communication channels open.

Affirm contributions. If someone is criticized (by you or anyone else – and however well you know they can take it) it can discourage others, who may avoid comments or questions that might be risky.

Remind the whole group about the agreed ground-rules if and when necessary.

Concerns about those who participate too much or too little can often be helped by changing the process and giving people a task in smaller groups. The shy get an opportunity to speak and the over-vociferous can't dominate the whole group.

When you subdivide during a session, always have at least three sub-groups in a room. If there are two groups they listen to each other and get distracted.

Ensure people know they can raise questions and how to do it appropriately. Question time can operate in different ways, e.g.:

(a) Have a 'questions board' where people can put up questions (possibly written on 'post-it' notes) as they occur to them. Have time planned to address these.

(b) Gather in small discussion groups to raise questions – some people feel more confident voicing queries in a small group. Others in the group may respond to some, and the group can select a key question to contribute to a plenary.

How to Use this Study

The Church Times Study Guides are designed to be a flexible resource that can be used in a number of ways. You could use them either individually or in a group, though they're likely to be more fun in a group. You could use the Guide for just one session, using it as a reading group or book club might, with everyone reading the whole thing at home, and then coming together to share responses and reviews. Or you could use the Guide as a kind of workbook for use within the group sessions, which is probably its best use. The number of sessions could vary as much as the group wants. The first two chapters are the main sections to this study, each of which is sufficient for at least one session. Depending on how seriously you take the reflections and tasks, each of the main sections could take several sessions to complete in fact. The third chapter is suitable for a 'wash-up' session, however you use the rest of the booklet. Through reflecting on a single passage, it pulls together some of the strands that are scattered through the other studies, and encourages the kind of reflection that might make a difference in your church.

Introduction
Writing Letters

Odd as it may seem, Christianity has actually decided that among its definitive holy texts there should be a collection of letters. Some of them are apparently quite mundane and personal, which makes it even odder. If you were devising a piece of sacred scripture or editing holy documents, would it occur to you to include the kind of letter that goes, more or less, 'Dear Tom, thinking about you all there. How's Flo? I'm feeling better now. Did I tell you I was in Ireland last week? Oh by the way Sean wants to be remembered to you ...' And so on. In among these kinds of detail are all sorts of information about the characters who inhabit the early churches and the issues that concern them. Scholars have been dissecting this information for generations, but sometimes you get the impression that they've forgotten that at heart these are letters, and that they've failed to notice just how odd that is.

But how do you study a letter? What do you need to know? If you were to pick up a letter on the doormat at home today how would you make sense of it? Perhaps you'd need to know who sent it, to whom they sent it, and why. It might help if you knew something about the sender or their situation. A letter sent from prison, for example, might have a particular character that would make it different from a card sent from holiday-makers on the Costa del Sol (though in my experience not necessarily so). Knowing our postal service, it helps sometimes to know when they sent it, and whether it belongs to a sequence of letters or if it's a reply to one you've sent. In essence these are the kinds of question which have accompanied the study of New Testament letters, and this study will look at some of the results.

When you begin to look at it, most of the New Testament actually consists of these letters. Although this is by no means a scientific comparison, there are 89 chapters of Gospels and 118 chapters of letters, for example (140 if you count Revelation). A large proportion of those letters was sent by Paul, an enigmatic figure sometimes credited with being the inventor of Christianity, even though he never met Jesus in the flesh. Certainly his writings have been enormously influential in the development of Christian ideas throughout the centuries. Some letters' authors remain unknown, the most that can be said being that they belong to a particular tradition, of Peter or John or Paul himself perhaps. Finally, the Revelation to John contains a series of letters that can only really be interpreted in the larger context of that book and its genre.

What makes this traditional study really compelling is the fact that a large proportion of the letters actually predate the Gospels, even though logically they follow them. Here we have the earliest writings of the Christian movement, giving us clues as to how the church developed in the way it did and how its theology came into being. Some of the latest writings in the New Testament are also to be found here giving us a chance to see how the nascent Christian community responded to changing circumstances, and giving us some insight, perhaps, into the kinds of personality that shaped the movement for centuries to come. Along the way we are enabled to share the concerns of ordinary people, with whom, perhaps, we can identify, and who are trying to find answers to the deeper questions of life and, on the basis of their faith, work out how to behave and what to belong to, even what to eat. We might even be surprised by how contemporary some of those issues are.

But beyond that, there are issues, as I've hinted, that are less well observed and commented on. For example:

- In study groups we are used to looking at specific letters or the letters of just one author. What issues emerge when we look at the letters as a whole?
- What is special about holy scripture in letter form? What do letters enable communicators to do that other forms would be less successful at?

- How does the process of writing letters fit into our evangelistic enter-prise: does it have a modern equivalent?

These are among the issues we shall address in this booklet. The first chapter will help us to read the letters using traditional questions, and prompting us to interrogate the letters for ourselves. The second chapter will look specifically at the 'new' questions outlined above – questions which derive from a curiosity about Christian communication and its processes. This will lead to the third chapter in which we reflect on Paul's description, in 2 Corinthians chapter 3, of the church itself as a letter. What are the implications of that description?

This is a study that connects us to the birth of a new faith community. You should approach it with a spirit of curiosity and adventure.

Reflection

Where else would you find a collection of letters? Perhaps you have a collection of letters from someone special tucked away somewhere, or perhaps you've come across a famous collection like Dietrich Bon-hoeffer's *Letters and Papers from Prison*.

Why do people keep letters? Here are some possible answers:

- Because the author is important (for example *The Collected Letters of D. H. Lawrence*)
- Because the occasion of the letters is important (for example, letters smuggled from prison)
- Because the content of the letters is important (for example, *The Screwtape Letters* by C. S. Lewis)

Which of these do you think is the most important with New Testament letters, or were they kept for some other reason?

1

Reading Letters

The job of scholars with regard to any part of scripture is to make sense of it, to try to discover the truth it contains, and to do so in a way that makes it useful for reflection and action in the church and in our lives today. This ought to be fairly easy when we are confronted with a collection of letters. Not many of us hear oracles. Religious poetry is a minority interest; and legendary storytelling is an uncommon art, but we all send and receive letters. And the way we approach New Testament letters is really no different from the way we would try to read any letter. We might first glance at the *date*, and certainly, if we were arranging a series of letters, date order would be very important.

Unfortunately none of the letters in the New Testament actually carries a date. In order to decide on the date of a letter, the curious enquirer has to undertake some detective work. The main lines of enquiry go like this.

1 From the accounts in Acts we can piece together a life of Paul, and indeed some kind of history of the early church. If we use this as a guide, then we can relate the small details contained in some of the letters to place them. There are problems with this approach. Acts is not a straightforward history. Like most history writing it is urging its readers to a point of view and is therefore selective in what it includes and sophisticated in its rhetoric. However, there is no reason to doubt the basic outline of events.

2 We are on shakier, more subjective ground, if we try to chart a development of Christian thinking, or a development in Paul's thinking, which is another line of approach. By determining a linear progression in thinking, often in conjunction with 1 above, it is thought possible to decide whereabouts on the line of development a particular piece of

writing falls. So commentators might regard 1 Thessalonians as a very undeveloped piece of writing, reflecting an early time when Christ's reappearance was an issue. Romans, on the other hand, might be considered much more developed, and from the end of Paul's ministry, when Acts reports that he lived in Rome.

3 A development of this method is to try to compare letters from Paul with letters from other people, to see how their theological ideas and agendas agree. This really becomes very subjective and often tells you more about the detective than anything. There is a further complication here, too, in that there is not absolute agreement about who wrote what. Some letters, which are claimed in their titles to be from Paul or Peter, are not regarded as actually being from their hand.

Reflection

To see how the processes work, and how difficult it is to reach a definitive view, you might like to read Philippians chapter 1. Verses 13, 17 and 20–26 suggest Paul was in prison and possibly facing death. We know from Acts 28.16 that Paul was held under house arrest in Rome, and that according to a later church historian he was executed there. Philippians 1.13 mentions a praetorian guard, which would fit a Rome setting. On these grounds we might think of a date in the early 60s. However, we know from 2 Corinthians 11.23 (unless this is just rhetoric), that Paul was imprisoned many times. Acts records an imprisonment in Caesarea, which would date the letter earlier, around 57–59. Ephesus is another possible location with strong support. Paul encountered lots of opposition there and Ephesus is comparitively close to Philippi. This might mean a date in the range 53–55. However, the thinking in Philippians is more mature than an early date would suggest.

From this you can see:

- how complicated a business it is
- how much personal judgement is involved
- how interconnected the problems are.

What we can say in general is that the letters of Paul were all written earlier than the first full Gospel (though the oral traditions which go to make up the Gospels were obviously in circulation in some form), and that the letters of Paul were probably the earliest we have.

The next question we might ask of our letter is, *who's it from?* You might think we'd be on stronger ground here, because most of the letters contain that information. However, ancient conventions were different from ours, and, apparently it was quite usual to claim that an apostle had written something, if the writing was in the tradition of that apostle. On the grounds of its content, language, and obvious relationship with the letter of Jude, 2 Peter is usually regarded as having been written around the turn of the first century, 30 or 40 years after that apostle's death, for example. More controversial are disputed letters of Paul. Few people now believe that Hebrews is genuinely from Paul, but there is robust debate about the so-called Pastoral Epistles: 1 and 2 Timothy and Titus, and especially Ephesians, which many people describe as coming from a generation after Paul, but in his theological tradition. Similar views can be found with regard to the letters of John. Clearly they belong in the same 'family' as the Gospel of John, but the exact authorship is disputed. The question we really need to ask is: does it matter?

Reflection

What does being sure about who is the author add to our understanding of a letter? In the early church, apostolic authorship conveyed authority and was a kind of kite mark of reassurance. Now that these works are firmly embedded in the canon of scripture, do we need that? It might be interesting to compare different works of Paul, but what difference does it make to know whether or not Peter wrote 1 Peter? We know next to nothing about some supposed authors anyway. Who was Jude? Which James, if any, wrote James? What do you think? If you get a letter from an organization, does it matter who signed it? In those circumstances, what matters more? Does thinking in this way help with the question, does it matter?

Of course, before we ask any of these questions we would probably glance at the address to make sure it's been delivered properly. So the next question might be *who are the addressees?* Whereas this is a relatively unimportant question with mail we might receive, it is one of the most important from the point of view of the New Testament, because it gives us insight into a further question: *why was the letter written?* and *what's it about?* One key characteristic of New Testament letters is that they are contextual. We can make clever guesses about where the communities were that the Gospels were written for, and even guess what circumstances led to each one being needed, but in the case of the letters we often know where they were written to; and, because some of them look rather like 'replies', we can have an idea of the issues in that particular place that the letter might address. Some things might perhaps follow from this.

- The issues in these young churches are surprisingly different. One of them might be concerned about sexual relations, and what we might now call Christian ethics, while another might be concerned with the appropriate response to perceived persecution. Yet another may have problems with deciding what is authentic in Christian worship, and so on.

- The letters show us a way of doing theology and developing theology that we might now call 'practical theology'. That is, theology is developed as a kind of conversation between traditions on the one hand, and actual situations and problems on the other.

- These letters are not a cover for 'dogma' or definitive universal responses. They are related to the situation that prompted them. That gives them a more 'accidental' feel.

- The traditions with which Paul, in particular, works are of two kinds. On the one hand we see the traditions of the Old Testament being reworked and reapplied. On the other, we see the beginnings of Christian traditions, which in some sense come 'from the Lord'. These traditions do have a different status from Paul's own application of them.

Reflection

Read 1 Corinthians chapters 10 and 11. In chapter 10 we see Paul working with and applying traditions about the Exodus. He manages to find connections between those traditions and:

- idolatry
- participation
- eating food that has been killed in a ritual way
- giving offence.

In chapter 11 we see a different kind of tradition in verse 23. This too is developed and applied in verses 27 and following. What do you think this might tell us about the way we use our own traditions? Can we still make new theology in the way Paul did? Do you think, as we read this kind of passage that we should be interested mainly in Paul's conclusions, or in the process that led to them?

Something that distinguishes questions about context and address from questions about authorship is that we have far more information available about the places to which the letters were sent, from independent contemporary sources and from archaeology. During the last 20 years or so, interest has grown in learning more about these places and especially about the social make-up of the communities. This can sometimes turn up information that challenges some of our assumptions. For example, James Dunn is of the view, using archaeological evidence, that the whole church in Corinth may have only amounted to no more than three or four dozen people. To read the letter with that in mind does (for me at least) cast it in a slightly different light.

New Testament scholars do ask other questions about the New Testament letters that are not usually appropriate for modern letters. They are interested in the editing process, for example. In some cases it appears that a number of different letters have been joined together in one document. Many people think that is the case with the Corinthian correspondence, others with 1 Peter. They are also interested when letters appear to be drawing on common material. Could it be that that gives us clues as to the existence of a body of material used, for example, for teaching new converts as a kind of catechism? There are great similarities between sections of 1 Peter and sections of Ephesians and Colossians, which have excited interest of this kind. Scholars are also suspicious that not everything that is sent, as it were, through the mail, is a letter. Sometimes these so-called letters are suspected to be sermons or homilies or liturgies dressed up as letters. Our interest is in the letters that look like letters and with which we can identify closely in modern parallel.

So having asked a few immediate questions about each of the letters, as we might of modern letters, what kind of information are we looking for, from the contents of the letters? What do we expect them to tell us? We have already decided that they are not a cover for 'dogma', though they do give us clues as to how the process of systematizing the Christian faith got started: that is, how it moved from stories and personal responsive letters, to creeds and doctrines. What we might legitimately expect is information about the processes of development. So we might look for clues as to how ministry or worship or theology were being understood at different times in different places, and the kinds of argument that supported views held, with the kinds of issues that prompted debate. We might expect to learn more about specific churches in terms of both practice and belief, and how they related to their context. We might add to what we can find out elsewhere about the context, and we might find out something more of the authors of the letters, and especially the role these letter-writers played in the growth and life of the whole.

Reflection

Look again at the paragraph above. Which of these possible areas would you consider the most fruitful for study today? If you are a member of a church, in what ways do you think that church could best use these works as a resource in its present situation?

2

Sending Letters

I have used the title, Sending Letters, to convey the approach to correspondence that sees it primarily as an act and form of communication. There are three questions, set out in the Introduction, that seem to me to arise from this approach. You will recall they are:

- In study groups we are used to looking at specific letters or the letters of just one author. What issues emerge when we look at the letters as a whole?
- What is special about holy scripture in letter form? What do letters enable communicators to do that would be less successful in other forms?
- How does the process of writing letters fit into our evangelistic enterprise: does it have a modern equivalent?

What we might expect to find in answer to the first question is, perhaps, something about news. Letters are often a means of conveying news, and we are speaking of a time, with regard to many of the letters, before Gospels appeared (ostensibly proclamations of news in a new and different form). The letters should be the first hint of news. The thing is, we've become accustomed to regarding as 'news' only what the Gospels mainly contain, that is, stories about Jesus. And so it is easy to disregard the letters as being news with the same status as Gospel. And yet they are the first indication of all that is new about this new religious phenomenon. Authors write in a new way about a new way of relating to God, and a new way of conducting or organizing religious life in this world. If there were one theme that does pervade these letters, it might be fair to say that it's: We're New!

And so, looking at the letters as a whole, we see that issues of identity are important. What's different about us? Letters often compare new Christians either with other religious expressions, or with their former pre-Christian selves. They do so not just to rubbish the opposition but also to help add to the emerging picture of what a Christian might look like and what a Christian church might look like in a positive and attractive way.

Reflection

You might like to look at a few Bible passages that make these comparisons. Ephesians 3.17–32 and Galatians 5.16–24 concentrate on behaviour, as does 1 Peter 2.9–10. Philippians 3.1–11contrasts Paul's past and present. Colossians 1.21–22 and 2.8–15 widen the discussion to include fundamental beliefs, as also 1 John 4.1–3. Hebrews 1.1–4 in a sense sums up the bottom line of Christian believing. What picture of 'newness' emerges from all this for you? If you were to write a statement of identity for the church based on these passages, which made no mention of the alternative, how would it read?

Questions of identity are related to believing different things, behaving in a different way as a consequence, and organizing religious expression in a different way too.

Questions about identity are also questions about relationships. What is the new relationship with God, and how was it made possible? What is an appropriate relationship with other religious expressions, and in particular the Jews? What is the right relationship with the state, and with national aspiration? Should Christians be distinguished by being set apart from the world, as you might suspect from reading the letters of John; or do they support the state and its legitimate functions through prayer, as you might think from reading Paul's letters?

A question that feels very contemporary is, how does this fledgling church deal with internal difference? The letters certainly do not present a picture of a golden age in which everyone agreed about everything –

indeed quite the reverse. Had there not been internal dispute and wrangling about important questions, most of the New Testament, let alone the letters, would never have been written. From these disputes we see emerge a strengthening idea of the difference between orthodoxy and heresy, and an idea of its relative importance. We see also the growth of an authority system, commending good order, discipline and accountability. Importantly we are able then to contextualize what is said, and read, with what is sometimes known as a 'hermeneutic of suspicion'. That is, we might ask to what extent the message has been dictated by events or pressures that are not immediately obvious, such as the threat of external harassment or internal discord. This way of reading encourages us to see the text as written from a particular point of view. In situations where the letters have in any case been written from situations of difference of opinion, we might reflect that what we have is the record of the winners, and that we only see the losers' arguments through their eyes. It is quite interesting to read a letter like 1 John, for example, and then imagine what it might have read like if those who are described as opponents had in fact won the day. But then, if we think about it, surely we expect letters to be written from a point of view. That is one of their usual features. A 'Letter from America' is not like a textbook on American geography or even a newspaper report about the week in America. It is a personal 'take'.

This might lead us to think about what else is special or different about letters as a form of communication. Letters are *dynamic*. They are often written in sequence as a situation develops. New Testament letters do not, generally, close debate but represent one stage within it. Like a modern chatroom there is opportunity for exchanges of views, and for each to spark off the other as theology develops. Letters *bear witness to relationships*. It is commonplace within Bible criticism nowadays to speak about 'the implied reader'. That is, what kind of person is this meant for and how is it written to commend itself to that particular audience? With the letters, the reader is openly acknowledged and known. A lot of the inconsequential chat in the letters of Paul, for example, bears witness at least to the fact that he knew to whom he was writing. Letters are *personal* in that sense. Paul writes to those he knows and who know him. The substance of the letters is about the difference the Risen Christ can make in their lives. There is a personal immediacy about all this that is best conveyed by letter. Another feature of letters is that they are *ordinary*. They deal with commonplace things and locate their theological reflection within those boundaries. They talk about diet, marriage, work, health and death – the stuff of ordinary concern. And of course they are *related to a context*: especially of the reader, but also of the writer. It is good to compare these New Testament letters with some later works from, say, the second century that bear the name letter, but which have lost all these characteristics. Instead of being dynamic they are closed and authoritarian; they are anonymous and general rather than personal and relational; they do not have a specific context, and they have lost all sense of the ordinary.

Reflection

Reading the preceding paragraphs with your own hermeneutic of suspicion, you will see that they have been written to commend letter writing as a form of gospel communication, but are they as good as all that? Might it not have been better simply to set out, in the form of 'A Beginner's Guide To …', all that is essential about Christian belief and practice? What would be lost in such an attempt, do you think?

I sometimes come across clergy who groan at the prospect of having to write a regular 'Letter' each week or month for some parish publication. Leaving aside the usefulness of such an exercise, it is clear that the New Testament letters are not written because someone expects them, or because it's a month since we wrote the last one. Their contents show that they are written for a reason. That 'occasional' sense is perhaps something that the letter form brings to the whole exercise.

Within the relationships that the letters describe, there are at least six reasons for writing them.

One is to *commend good practice*. That is something which a letter is well suited to. When we see good practice we want to respond straight away, and tell others with whom we are in contact. We see Paul, for example, commending the innovative practice of the church in Macedonia in 2 Corinthians 8. We see him commending particular forms of worship, as in 1 Corinthians 11, and in the letter to Philemon we see Paul trying to persuade Philemon to take back his runaway slave as an example of good practice.

Reflection

Read Revelation chapters 2 and 3. These contain seven letters to different churches, which some scholars think circulated together and were meant to be read as examples of good and bad practice. Which of these churches had nothing to commend it and which had everything?

Another function of the letters is *to encourage*. Christians were extremely vulnerable, coming under suspicion both from the state, civil authorities and other religious groups. In some instances, to become a Christian was to opt out of civic life. The Greek word for 'encouragement' is *paraklesis,* which also means comfort and consolation. Paul is particularly keen to encourage. Philippians 1.3–11 is one example. The whole of the letter to the Hebrews (though probably not by Paul) is an attempt to encourage and reinspire a congregation whose faith and enthusiasm has flagged. Written to those who experienced suffering of some kind, 1 Peter is a message of support and encouragement that they are following truly in the steps of Christ. And so, in a wider sense, the letters are *a means of pastoral support.* At the very least they show a concern for oversight. Theology sometimes develops within this pastoral framework (for example, as noted above in 1 Peter) as authors attempt to make sense of suffering, hardship and defeat. The letters have a role in *maintaining fellowship.* The writers seem at pains to give a sense of the wider church, and to describe themselves as a kind of link between congregations. The letters are a *means of teaching,* as situations demand a response, and as we have seen, they are *vehicles of dialogue,* enabling conversations and ideas to develop.

If these are among the things that letters do, and do specially in the New Testament, the next question is: where are these functions maintained in our own evangelistic enterprise? As we attempt to be bearers of news, how and where does that correspond to our roles as commenders of good practice, encouragers, pastoral supports, those who maintain fellowship, teachers and enablers of dialogue? And underlying all this, where is the mechanism which facilitates all this in the context of church speaking to church, as in the letters? The most obvious answers are perhaps:

- National Christian press
- Local community Christian press
- Religious broadcasting
- Ecumenical initiatives.

Reflection

Try to get hold of copies of different religious newspapers. These tend to be denomination based, and sometimes cater for a specific constituency within a denomination. See if you can find evidence of the six functions listed above in the paper you chose. That should be fairly easy. But see how they encourage, how they teach and commend good practice etc. The very fact of having a newspaper at all could be said to be encouraging in that it gives a sense of belonging to something bigger than the local, which shows signs of success somewhere. Bearing in mind our current study, what do you think is the role of the letters page, and how successful is your chosen publication in achieving its purpose? You might like to reflect on the other suggestions above. Have they got more potential than newspapers, do you think, to maintain the traditions of the letters?

What this part of the study has asked us to do, is to think of the letters as vehicles of communication, and to work from our experience of letters nowadays to see how that communication operates. This has led us to ask questions that are not normally asked as we approach the letters from a different perspective. This search for different ways of reading Bible texts is very much in vogue at the moment. It is a reaction against seeing texts, like the letters, as being essentially historical documents whose secrets are to be unlocked by historical experts using the methods that such people commonly employ. Readers nowadays are encouraged to build upon historical insights, using their own experience and context as a key to unlocking meaning, in an adventurous and even playful way.

3

The Open Letter

While we are looking in this general way at letters, and how to read them, it would be remiss not to reflect on an intriguing passage in 2 Corinthians 3. This is what Paul says:

> You yourselves are our letter, written in our hearts, that everyone can read and understand; and it is plain that you are a letter from Christ, entrusted to our care, written not with ink but with the Spirit of the living God; not on stone tablets but on the tablets of human hearts.
>
> (verses 2 and 3, New Jerusalem Bible)

It is surely notable that Paul speaks about the church as an open letter, and considers that to be both a legitimate and a useful description. Perhaps some of the work we have done in this study will help us to throw further light on the passage.

- To describe the church as an act of communication is very encouraging for those of us who believe that communication lies at the heart of the theological task, and that that task is best worked out at local level where Christian tradition is reflected upon in response to the needs of a local context. This whole letter culture is not about dogma and doctrine. It is about reflective conversation within a communicating relationship. To see the church described like that by Paul is a useful corrective to less dynamic views or more hierarchical views.
- If we were right in identifying six of the functions of a letter in the preceding study, then perhaps we should ask if those functions should not also be evident in the church. In other words, ought it not to be

the case that the church should consider itself working authentically when it is working to identify good practice; when it is encouraging, teaching, offering pastoral support and enabling theology to develop through dialogue.

- The way that Paul develops his point makes it clear that he believes that a key feature of letters is their personal and relational character. He wants to say that letters convey the personality of their authors, and that the author of the letter which is the church in Corinth is God himself. The main implication of the view is that people should be able to see something of the character of God when they see the church. We are accustomed to telling people that if they want to see what the church *is* they should see what the church *does*. This takes that approach a stage further.

- The church as letter of Christ is an unfamiliar and unusual picture. We are much more accustomed to talking about the Body of Christ. Both pictures offer us a challenge to continuity. The Body of Christ picks up from the Gospel narratives and, minimally, challenges us to do as Jesus did. The 2 Corinthians image picks up from the letters and challenges us to continue to be a letter of Christ, with all that involves.

- This letter is an open letter, something that 'everyone can read and understand', and so invites us to think about evangelism. Just as a letter is an appropriate way for church to speak to church; so it is an appropriate way to understand how the church speaks to the world. The further implication is that this letter is 'plain', it is transparent; and communicates to the world whether intentionally or otherwise.

Reflection

How well do you think the words 'open' and 'transparent' sit with the word 'church' in your experience? You might like to think about the way the church is organized. Perhaps you might think about how clear the objectives of your church really are. Do you, for example, have a mission statement, and if so, who devised it and how often is it revisited or reviewed and by whom? Or you might like to think about how obvious the church's aims and objectives are to those unfamiliar with church life. Is the letter that is your church written in a foreign language?

Imagine yourself standing outside a church in a high street on a busy day and asking passers-by, 'What do you think goes on here?' What kind of answers do you think you would get from those unfamiliar with church? How might they reach their answers – what clues would they find?

What would be involved in organizing an Open Day for your church? What kinds of stall and exhibit would you have? What would be the programme for the day? How would you assess its success?

To think about letters in the way we have inevitably leads to challenges about the way we view the biblical text, the way we view the task of evangelism, and the way we describe the church. Letters were an innovative form of holy writ, and those who wrote them would no doubt be amazed at the use to which they have been put. This study has tried to work with that innovation and its consequences, and to help us to see that after all, and still, 'We're new!'

4

Further Reading

This study crosses a number of disciplines, and I am unaware of any work that picks up the thread from exactly where we've left it. My book *Communication and The Gospel* (Darton, Longman & Todd, 2002) sets this study in a wider context of communication.

If you are looking for books about the letters, a good place to start is H. Marshall, S. Travis and I. Paul, *Exploring the New Testament, Vol 2 The Letters and Revelation* (SPCK, 2002), which contains accessible and solid scholarship on all the letters.

If social description and social-scientific criticism looks as if it might interest you, then J. H. Elliott, *What is Social Scientific Criticism?* (Fortress, 1993) is as good a place as any to start.

As an introduction to Paul, I like D. Horrell, *An Introduction to the Study of Paul* (Continuum, 2000).

One to request from the library perhaps is D. Burkett, *An Introduction to the New Testament and the Origins of Christianity* (Cambridge University Press, 2002).

However, it may be that the most appropriate kind of book for further reflection would be one of the crop that is looking at what the church might be, and become in these times of fresh expressions. *The Mission Shaped Church* (Church House, 2003) is the obvious place to start.